G000292692

C. Collins
Published by Collins   Collins® is a registered trademark of HarperCollins Publishers Limited
An imprint of HarperCollins Publishers   Copyright © HarperCollins Publishers Ltd 2009
77-85 Fulham Palace Road, Hammersmith, London W6 8JB   www.harpercollins.co.uk

Mapping generated from Collins Bartholomew digital databases

Pages 4-5 & 54-79 use map data licensed from Ordnance Survey® with the permission of the Controller
of Her Majesty's Stationery Office. © Crown copyright. Licence number 399302

The grid on the mapping on pages 4-5 & 54-79 is the National Grid taken from the Ordnance Survey map
with the permission of the Controller of Her Majesty's Stationery Office.

Printed in China   ISBN 978-0-00-727438-3   Imp 001   VI12388   RDA

e-mail:roadcheck@harpercollins.co.uk

courtesy of Edinburgh & Lothians Tourist Board

Edinburgh Castle ☼ ♿ 4 **A1** & 69 **C2**

Edinburgh Castle rises from an extinct volcanic outcrop and dominates the city that has grown up around it. In its early years the castle was a royal residence although in less troubled times the Palace of Holyroodhouse (see page 6) was preferred for its comfort. In 1566 the castle saw Mary, Queen of Scots give birth to James VI. He became king one year later (also crowned James I of England in 1603). Visit the Stone of Destiny and the 'Honours of the Kingdom' (the Scottish Crown Jewels and Regalia) which are both kept in the Crown Room at the Royal Palace. Since the reign of James IV it has assumed an increasingly military role. The 6 ton Mons Meg cannon, if still working today, could fire its stones and reach the Botanic Gardens 2 miles (3.2 km) away. To see a gun in action (except Sundays) watch the master gunner on the Mills Mount Battery with the One o'clock gun; fired almost every day since 1851. Take a quieter moment in St.Margaret's chapel, Edinburgh's oldest building, or in the Dog Cemetery where mascots and officers' pets have been laid to rest here since the 1840s. Open daily.

Adults £12, concessions available.

Castlehill ☎ 0131 225 9846

www.edinburghcastle.gov.uk

• Audio tours and guidebooks
Choose to listen in English, French, German, Spanish, Italian, Japanese, Russian or Mandarin when you hire a headset to lead you around.
Adults £3.50, concessions available.
A "Thirty Steps to History" illustrated guidebook follows a trail through the castle.
Guidebooks £4.95, available in English, French and Japanese

- Guided tours

Meet a castle steward near the Argyle Battery for an outside complimentary tour which lasts about 25 minutes and finishes near the Palace in Crown Square. Then go on to discover the buildings on your own. Tours are given throughout the day but subject to the weather and availability so ask when entering the castle.

- Refreshments

The Redcoat Café (in the old Cart Shed) is named after the distinctive uniform of the castle guard; a self-service café with spectacular views. The Queen Anne Café is located at the top of the Castle next to the Great Hall offering an elegant contemporary space with table service.

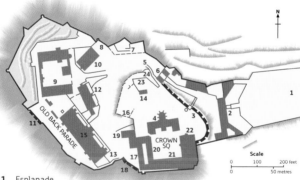

1 Esplanade
2 Gatehouse
3 Forewall & Half Moon Batteries
4 Scottish National War Memorial
5 Lang Stairs
6 Argyle Tower & Portcullis Gate
7 Argyle Battery
8 Mills Mount Battery
9 National War Museum of Scotland
10 Cart Shed (Café)
11 Butts Battery
12 Governor's House
13 Royal Scots Dragoon Guards Regimental Museum
14 St. Margaret's Chapel
15 New Barracks
16 Foog's Gate
17 Military Prison
18 Durys Battery
19 Royal Scots Regimental Museum
20 Queen Anne Building
21 The Great Hall
22 The Royal Palace
23 Mons Meg Cannon
24 Dog Cemetery

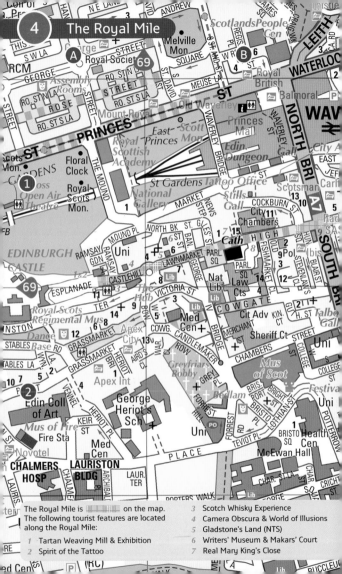

The Royal Mile is ▢▢▢▢▢ on the map.
The following tourist features are located
along the Royal Mile:

1 Tartan Weaving Mill & Exhibition
2 Spirit of the Tattoo

3 Scotch Whisky Experience
4 Camera Obscura & World of Illusions
5 Gladstone's Land (NTS)
6 Writers' Museum & Makars' Court
7 Real Mary King's Close

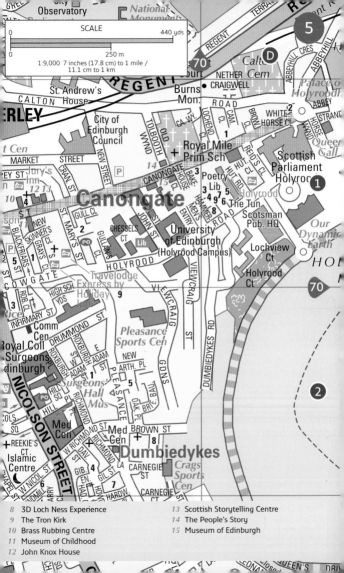

Palace of Holyroodhouse ♿

5 D1 & 70 B2

Largely a 17th century building, the north-west tower was built in 1501 for James IV. Holyroodhouse is the Queen's official residence in Scotland and is used for state ceremonies. The Great Gallery occupies the whole of the first floor of the north wing and in it hangs 89 portraits of real and legendary kings of Scotland. The state apartments reflect the changing tastes of successive monarchs and are renowned for their fine stucco ceilings. Mary, Queen of Scots' chambers are in the west corner tower.

Open daily, although opening times may be subject to change at short notice.

Adults £9.80, concessions available.

Canongate ☎ 0131 556 5100

www.royalcollection.org.uk

● Audio tours

An audio tour is included in the admission price and is available in English, French, German, Italian, Spanish and Japanese. A family audio tour and activity trail is also available in English.

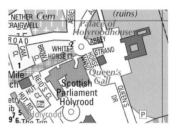

● Guidebooks

Guidebooks are available in English.

● Exclusive guided tours for individuals

At least one evening per month from May to September, the Palace has guided tours (when it is closed to the general public). The history of the palace is rich with it being used by Bonnie Prince Charlie during the 1745 uprising to the present day with events such as the famous garden parties. What will an expert show you? These 18.30 summer evening tours include a copy of the official guidebook, 20% discount in the Royal Collection shop (which is opened especially) and end with a glass of champagne.

Adults £30. Limited availability. Must be pre-booked.

Tours 0131 558 1700.

Guided private tours for groups can be arranged all year round.

● Special interest talks

Choose between the turbulent life of Mary, Queen of Scots or the world famous collection of tapestries. Tea or coffee is followed by an expert guides' talk and an audio tour of the Palace.

Tues, Wed and Thurs between March to December (excluding August).

Adults £13.95, concessions available.

Limited availability; maximum of 30 per tour (minimum of 15).

• Family activities ☼
During school holidays and weekends the kids can 'drop in' for
activities designed for 5 – 11 year olds (and their parents!...
compulsory since the children must be accompanied). Standard
admission prices apply, with all materials provided free of charge but
once you've purchased a palace ticket you can come back as many
times as you like, in a year, for free. Their website has details.

• Café at the Palace
In the historic setting of the Palace's Mews Courtyard this café
escapes the noise of the city and offers a changing menu of freshly
prepared lunches but also offers light snacks. It can be used without
visiting the palace itself.
Open every day in the summer from 10am to 6pm.

The Royal Collection © 2008, Her Majesty Queen Elizabeth II

Queen's Gallery (Palace of Holyroodhouse) ♿   **5 D1** & **70 B2**
The Gallery hosts a programme of changing exhibitions from the
Royal Collection, focusing primarily on works from the Royal Library
at Windsor Castle.
Open daily, although opening times may be subject to change at
short notice.
Adults £5, concessions available.
Canongate

• Combined visit
A joint ticket with The Queen's Gallery Adults £13, concessions
available.

Edinburgh has superb architecture, medieval streets, pleasant gardens, great museums, wide open spaces and Georgian Terraces and as you walk the streets there is a real sense of history.

Dominating the skyline is Edinburgh Castle sitting on its crag above the city. From the castle The Royal Mile runs east to the Palace of Holyroodhouse. The Royal Mile runs through the heart of the Old Town and numerous cobbled wynds and cramped closes lead off it. To the north of Princes Street lies the New Town, combining Georgian crescents, squares and circuses to form one of Europe's best examples of Georgian town planning.

Guide to symbols

♿ Disabled facilities available (but some areas may still be restricted). Venues without this symbol may still have facilities. Always check before travelling.

◯ Edinburgh is full of fascinating things for children to see and do. This guide suggests some of them with this symbol.

This symbol gives an indication of some of Edinburgh's best known attractions. They are places not to miss on your trip to Edinburgh.

This symbol means there is no charge if you have an Edinburgh Pass, see below for details.

Map references (e.g. **75 D2**) are provided for most places. All other places can be located using the street address, unless otherwise stated.

Edinburgh Pass

Purchase a one, two or three day pass for free entry to over 30 top attractions, free bus travel and offers from restaurants, shops and leisure facilities.
Purchase online or from one of the tourist information centres.
One day £24 (children 5-15 £16), two days £36 (£24) and three days £48 (£32).
www.edinburgh.org/pass

Visitor attractions

Edinburgh has a whole host of attractions to visit, many of them alongside the Royal Mile. The majority of the attractions have longer opening hours during the Festival.

3D Loch Ness Experience
Key number 8, **4 B1**

Does Nessie really exist? This is your turn to be the judge. There are photos, illusions, hoaxes and eye witness accounts shown in a 25 minute performance, headsets and 3D glasses supplied! Listen in 5 different languages.
Open daily.
Adults £5.95, concessions available.
1 Parliament Square ☎ 0131 225 2290
www.3dlochness.com

Arthur's Seat
77 D1

The core of an extinct volcano, Arthur's Seat rises 251m (822 feet) above sea level. From the top there are superb views across much of Edinburgh and the Firth of Forth. The easiest walk up to the summit is from the car park beside Dunsapie Loch.
Holyrood Park

Brass Rubbing Centre ☼
Key number 10, **5 C1**

Housed in Trinity Apse, all that remains of the Gothic Holy Trinity Collegiate Church, the centre has replicas of ancient Pictish crosses, medieval church brasses and rare Scottish brasses from which rubbings can be taken.
Open Mon-Sat from April to September, also Sundays in August.
Free, but there is a charge to make a rubbing.
Trinity Apse, Chalmer's Close ☎ 0131 556 4364
www.cac.org.uk

Camera Obscura and World of Illusions
Key number 4, **4 A1**

Live panoramic views of the city beamed via a lens into the auditorium. The best views are at noon on a bright day. There are hands-on activities and exhibitions on pinhole photography and holography and fine views over the city from the rooftop terrace.
Open daily.
Adults £7.95, concessions available.
Castlehill ☎ 0131 226 3709
www.camera-obscura.co.uk

City Art Centre ♿
4 B1

Home to the city's collection of Scottish Art, around 3,500 paintings, watercolours, drawings, prints, photographs, sculptures and tapestries. Contemporary works are continually being added. There are many temporary exhibitions of art.
Open daily.
Free. Charge for some temporary exhibitions.
2 Market Street ☎ 0131 529 3993
www.cac.org.uk

Dean Gallery ♿   67 **D2**

Houses a huge collection of work by the distinguised Scottish Sculptor, Eduardo Paolazzi, and the Dada and Surrealist collections from the Gallery of Modern Art. The gallery can be reached from the attractive Water of Leith walkway.

Open daily.

Free. Charge for some temporary exhibitions.

73 Belford Road   ☎ 0131 624 6200

www.nationalgalleries.org

Dynamic Earth ⌚ ♿   see **Our Dynamic Earth**, page 14

Edinburgh Castle ⌚ ♿   see pages 2-3

Edinburgh Dungeon ♿   4 **B1**

Scotland's bloody past is brought to life by actors, rides and tableaux in the dungeons buried beneath Edinburgh's pavements. This attraction is not for young children or those of a nervous disposition!

Open daily.

Adults £12.95, concessions available.

31 Market Street   ☎ 01303 816077

www.thedungeons.com

Georgian House (NTS)   68 **B2**

Three floors of the Georgian House are elegantly furnished as they would have been by the Lamont family, the first owners of the house, in 1796.

Open daily, March to November.

Adults £5, concessions available.

7 Charlotte Square   ☎ 0844 493 2118

www.nts.org.uk

Gladstone's Land (NTS)   *Key number 5,* 4 **B1**

A superb example of a 17th century tenement house. Sensitively restored to give a feeling of life here in the 1600s.

Open daily, March to October.

Adults £5, concessions available.

477b Lawnmarket   ☎ 0844 493 2120

www.nts.org.uk

Glasshouse Experience ♿   62 **B1**

A series of ten glasshouses with five climatic zones to suit plants from all over the world. Built in 1852 the Temperate Palm House is still Britain's tallest at approximately 23 metres. Also see Royal Botanic Gardens of Edinburgh.

Open daily.

Adults £3.50, concessions available.

Royal Botanic Garden, Edinburgh, Inverleith Row   ☎ 0131 552 7171

www.rbge.org.uk

Greyfriars Bobby 4 **B2**
This faithful Skye Terrier watched over
the grave of his master, John Gray, for
14 years after Gray's death in 1858.
Cared for by locals, Bobby lived happily
until 1872, never spending a night away
from his master's grave. The statue was
erected soon after Bobby's death.
Greyfriars Place
www.greyfriarsbobby.co.uk

courtesy of Rosemary MacLeod

Holyrood Park 71 **C2**
A 263ha (650 acre) oasis of peace in the
very heart of the city. The park features
an amazing variety of landscapes:
mountains, crags, moorland, marshes,
glens, lochs and fields. Also see Arthur's Seat.
www.historic-scotland.gov.uk
☎ 0131 556 1761

John Knox House ⅙ see **Scottish Storytelling Centre**, page 18

Linlithgow Palace out of map area
Magnificent ruined medieval castle and grounds on the side of
Linlithgow Loch (outside Edinburgh but worth a visit). Once home to
the royal court and most of the Stewart kings of Scotland. Birthplace
of James V (1512) and Mary, Queen of Scots (1542). There are still
corridors and halls to stroll along, with a courtyard and its fountain
built by James V, which flows every Sunday in July and August. The
palace was left ablaze in 1746 at the end of the Jacobite Rising.
Open daily. £5.20, concessions available.
Linlithgow, west of Edinburgh.
☎ 01506 842896

Museum of Childhood ☼ ⅙ *Key number 11*, 5 **C1**
Devoted to the history of childhood, this is an enchanting, colourful
and noisy place. Dolls, trains, models, games and books from all over
the world crowd the rooms.
Open daily.
Free.
42 High Street ☎ 0131 529 4142
www.cac.org.uk

Museum of Edinburgh *Key number 15*, 5 **C1**
Huntly House itself has a wealth of original fittings, panelling and
fireplaces. It was opened in 1932 as the principal city museum. The
exhibits and period room settings give a great insight into the past life
of Edinburgh.
Open Mon-Sat (also Sundays during August). Free
142 Canongate ☎ 0131 529 4143
www.cac.org.uk

National Gallery of Scotland ♿   4 A1

Houses Scotland's greatest collections of European paintings and
sculpture from the Renaissance to Post-Impressionism. Includes works
by Velazquez, El Greco, Turner, Constable and Van Gogh.
Open daily. Late night opening on Thurs.
Free. Charge for some temporary exhibitions.
The Mound   ☎ 0131 624 6200
www.nationalgalleries.org

National Library of Scotland ♿   4 B1

Scotland's largest reference library only available to academics.
Various exhibitions are open to all. Contact the library for details.
Exhibitions open daily.
Free.
George IV Bridge   ☎ 0131 623 3700
www.nls.uk

National Museum of Scotland ☀ ♿   4 B2

Collections telling the story of
Scotland – past, present and
future. Scotland's land, people
and culture, the influence the
world has had on Scotland and
Scotland has had on the world.
All the collections have tales to
tell; Viking brooches, Pictish
stones, ancient chessmen and
Queen Mary's clarsach. Connect
with Dolly the sheep, design a
robot, test drive a Formula One
car or blast off into outer space.

courtesy of Rosemary MacLeod

Part of the Victorian Royal
Museum is now closed until
2011 while 16 new galleries,
a learning centre, two hands-
on discovery areas and better
visitor facilities are installed.
For more information visit
www.nms.ac.uk/royalmuseumproject

Open daily
Free. Charge for some
temporary exhibitions.
Chambers Street
www.nms.ac.uk   ☎ 0131 225 7534

National Gallery of Scotland

courtesy of Rosemary MacLeod

National War Museum of Scotland ♿   69 **C2**
The Museum explores the Scottish experience of war and military service over the last 400 years. Different aspects of Scottish military history are explored in six thematic galleries.
Open daily.
Admission is included in the cost of £12 to enter the castle.
Edinburgh Castle, Castlehill   ☎ 0131 247 4413
www.nms.ac.uk   www.edinburghcastle.gov.uk

Nelson Monument   70 **A1**
Monument to Admiral Nelson who was victorious at the Battle of Trafalgar. The tower is shaped like a telescope, with a timeball on the top which is lowered as the one o'clock gun from Edinburgh Castle is fired. There are spectacular views from the top of the tower, reached by 143 steps.
Open Mon-Sat. £3.
Calton Hill   ☎ 0845 2255 121
www.cac.org.uk

Newhaven Heritage Museum   57 **D1**
Situated in the historic fishmarket at Newhaven Harbour, this lively museum tells the story of Newhaven and its people. Reconstructed sets of fishwives and fishermen and first hand accounts of their lives.
Open daily. Free.
Pier Place   ☎ 0131 551 4165
www.cac.org.uk

No. 28 Charlotte Square (NTS) ♿ **68 B2**
The headquarters of the National Trust for Scotland is here and there is an exhibition about the NTS and its work. The Drawing Room Gallery has a collection of 20th century Scottish paintings, regency furniture and *objets d'art*. There is a shop and coffee house.
Open Mon-Sat. Gallery open Mon-Fri 11am-3pm.
Free.
28 Charlotte Square ☎ 0131 243 9300
www.nts.org.uk

Our Dynamic Earth ☺ ♿ **5 D1**
Ten themed areas, full of surprises and intriguing facts using dramatic special effects, stunning imagery and state-of-the-art interactive displays to take the visitor on a journey of discovery from the very beginning of time to our unknown future.
Open daily.
Adults £9.50, concessions available.
Holyrood Road ☎ 0131 550 7800
www.dynamicearth.co.uk

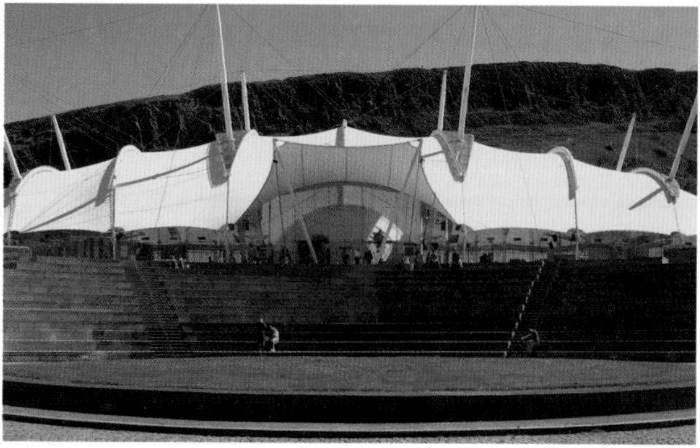

courtesy of Sonia Dawkins

Palace of Holyroodhouse ♿ see pages **6-7**

People's Story ♿ *Key number 14,* **5 C1**
A lively museum which uses oral history, reminiscence, and written sources to tell the story of the lives, work and leisure of the ordinary people of Edinburgh, from the late 18th century to the present day.
Open Mon-Sat & Sun during August. Free.
Canongate Tolbooth, 163 Canongate ☎ 0131 529 4057
www.cac.org.uk

Queen's Gallery (Palace of Holyroodhouse) ♿ see pages **6-7**

Real Mary King's Close   *Key number 7,* **4 B1**
Some of the Old Town's closes were originally narrow streets with houses on either side (tenements) stretching up to seven storeys high. In 1753, the Burgh Council decided to develop a new building on this site (now the City Chambers) and the remnants of Mary King's Close was left beneath the building. Visitors are guided underground by one of the characters from the past to see an historically accurate interpretation of life here from the 16th-19th centuries.
Open daily, with tours every 20 minutes.
Adults £9.50, concessions available. Pre-booking is essential.
2 Warriston's Close, off Royal Mile   ☎ 08702 430 160
www.realmarykingsclose.co.uk

Royal Botanic Garden Edinburgh ♿
62 B2

The Botanics are acknowledged to be some of the finest gardens in the world where beautiful and unusual plants can be found. There are ten themed glasshouses (see Glasshouse Experience), the Chinese Hillside, Rock Garden, Scottish Heath Garden and an arboretum with over 200 species of tree. Open daily. Free. Glasshouses £3.50. Guided tours available April to September £3.
Inverleith Row   ☎ 0131 552 7171
www.rbge.org.uk

Royal Mile   see pages **4-5**
Sloping gently from the castle to the Palace of Holyroodhouse, the Royal Mile is a crowded, historic and romantic jumble of buildings from past centuries and is the tourist hub of Edinburgh.

courtesy of Rosemary MacLeod

Castlehill, Lawnmarket, High Street and Canongate
www.edinburgh-royalmile.com

Royal Scots Dragoon Guards Regimental Museum   **69 C3**
(Edinburgh Castle) ♿
The museum which traces the roots of Scotland's only Cavalry Regiment back to 1678.
Open daily.
Admission is included in the cost of £12 to enter the castle.
Edinburgh Castle, Castlehill   ☎ 0131 310 5102
www.scotsdgmuseum.com   www.edinburghcastle.gov.uk

Royal Scots Regimental Museum (Edinburgh Castle)   4 A2
Housed in a 1900 Drill Hall, this museum contains memorabilia illustrating the Regiment's illustrious history.
Open daily.
Admission is included in the cost of £12 to enter the castle.
Edinburgh Castle, Castlehill   ☎ 0131 310 5018
www.theroyalscots.co.uk   www.edinburghcastle.gov.uk

Royal Scottish Academy &   4 A1
The RSA Annual Exhibition is held here in May and June and there are other temporary exhibitions during the rest of the year.
Opening varies with exhibitions.
Prices vary with exhibitions.
The Mound   ☎ 0131 225 6671
www.royalscottishacadamy.org

Royal Yacht Britannia &   58 B1
For 44 years the Royal Yacht served the Queen and royal family, and was used for state visits, diplomatic functions and royal holidays.
Visits begin in the visitor centre where there are exhibits, displays and

courtesy of Rosemary MacLeod

photographs before roaming the ship with an audio handset. The bridge, the admiral's quarters, the officers' mess and the state apartments can all be viewed. Open daily. Pre-booking advisable during August. Adult £9.75, concessions available. Ocean Terminal Level 2, Leith
☎ 0131 555 5566
www.royalyachtbritannia.co.uk

Scotch Whisky Heritage Centre &   *Key number 3,* 4 A2
Illustrates the history of Scotch Whisky as well as providing a tour of the whisky making process. Open daily.
Adult £9.50, concessions available.
354 Castlehill   ☎ 0131 220 0441
www.whisky-heritage.co.uk

Scott Monument 🕯   4 B1
A monument to Sir Walter Scott built in 1844 and decorated with figures from his novels. There are panoramic views from the top, a leg-wearying 287 steps above ground level.
Open daily. £3.
East Princes Street Gardens   ☎ 0131 529 4068
www.cac.org.uk

Scottish National Gallery of Modern Art ♿   67 **C2**
Set in beautiful parkland, which includes a sculpture garden, this is a superb collection of 20th century paintings, graphic art and sculpture. The gallery can be reached from the Water of Leith walkway.
Open daily.
Free. Charge for some temporary exhibitions.
75 Belford Road   ☎ 0131 624 6200
www.nationalgalleries.org

Scottish National Portrait Gallery ♿
                                 69 **D1**

Provides a unique visual history of Scotland, told through portraits of the figures who shaped it: royals and rebels, poets and philosophers, heroes and villains. The portraits are all of Scots but not all are by Scots. The gallery is also home to the Scottish National Photography Collection.
Open daily.
Free. Charge for some temporary exhibitions.
1 Queen Street   ☎ 0131 624 6200
www.nationalgalleries.org

courtesy of Rosemary MacLeod

Scottish Parliament, Holyrood ♿   5 **D1**
The public galleries of the Chamber or Committee room are open on business days and on non-business days the rooms themselves are accessible by visitors. There's an exhibition about the parliament and guided tours are available on non-business days.
Free admission to the building, exhibition and public galleries.
Guided tours £6, concessions available.   ☎ 0131 348 5200
www.scottish.parliament.uk

courtesy of Sonia Dawkins

Scottish Storytelling Centre & John Knox House &

Key number 13 & 12, **5 C1**

Discover live oral storytelling with their seasonal programme. Includes the Netherbow Theatre and a licensed Cafe.

• John Knox House dates from the end of the 15th century and is the only one of this era remaining on the Royal Mile. It was lived in by James Mosman, jeweller and goldsmith to Queen Mary and by John Knox the Scottish religious reformer. There is an exhibition about both men and a reconstruction of the goldsmith's workbench.

Open Mon-Sat (also Sundays in July and August).

courtesy of Rosemary MacLeod

Free exhibition. Charge for events.
Charge for house: Adults £3.50, concessions available.
43 High Street ☎ 0131 556 9579
www.scottishstorytellingcentre.co.uk

Seafari Adventures: High Speed Boat Trips &

57 C1

An exhilarating 1hr discovery on the Firth of Forth in a rigid inflatable boat. Wear warm clothing but if it is sunny then bring sunglasses and cream. Waterproofs supplied. Meet at the Newhaven lighthouse.
Open daily, April to October.
Adults £20, concessions available. Booking essential.
Newhaven Harbour, Leith ☎ 0131 331 4857
www.seafari.co.uk

Spirit of the Tattoo Visitor Centre &

Key number 2, **4 A1**

An interactive exhibition and movie theatre allows visitors to experience the sights and sounds of the Edinburgh Tattoo all year round (the event itself takes place in August, see page 40).
Open daily. Free.
33-34 Market Street ☎ 0131 225 8616
www.edinburgh-tattoo.co.uk/spirittattoo/

St. Giles Cathedral &

4 B1

Not strictly a cathedral but the historical title has stuck, maybe because of its prominent position on the High Street. Renowned for its hollow-crown tower, stained glass, Rieger organ and beautiful Thistle Chapel.
Open daily.
Free, visitors are, however, invited to make a £2 donation.
High Street ☎ 0131 225 9442
www.stgilescathedral.org.uk

St. Mary's Episcopal Cathedral ♿   **68 A3**
Built in the 1870s by Sir George Gilbert Scott, this is a huge neo-gothic church with three spires.
Open daily. Free.
Palmerston Place   ☎ 0131 225 6293
www.cathedral.net

Stills Gallery ♿   **4 B1**
Photographic gallery of Scottish and international contemporary photographers.
Open daily. Free.
23 Cockburn Street   ☎ 0131 622 6200
www.stills.org

Surgeons' Hall Museum ♿   **5 C2**
Explore the history of surgery in Edinburgh and further afield and view the significant dental collection. The Pathology Museum, closed during exam periods, displays the largest collection of pathological anatomy in the UK. Temporary medical related exhibitions.
Open Mon-Fri, noon-4pm.
Adults £5.
Nicolson Street   ☎ 0131 527 1649
www.rcsed.ac.uk

Talbot Rice Gallery ♿   **4 B2**
Georgian gallery exhibiting Edinburgh University's collection of old master paintings and bronzes. Also a contemporary gallery showing up to seven exhibitions per year.
Open Tue-Sat. Free.
University of Edinburgh, Old College Quad, South Bridge
www.trg.ed.ac.uk   ☎ 0131 650 2210

Tartan Weaving Mill and Exhibition ♿   *Key number 1,* **4 A1**
Housed in a building that used to contain the reservoir that supplied the water to the residents of the Royal Mile. Visitors can dress in ancient Scottish costume and be photographed and also learn about the history of Scotland's National Dress.
Open daily. Free.
555 Castlehill, Royal Mile   ☎ 0131 226 1555
www.geoffreykilts.co.uk/tartanweavingmill.htm

Writers' Museum and Makars' Court   *Key number 6,* **4 B1**
Situated in Lady Stair's House. Dedicated to the lives and work of Scotland's great literary figures, in particular Robert Burns, Sir Walter Scott, and Robert Louis Stevenson. Makars' Court has inscriptions commemorating famous Scottish writers.
Open Mon-Sat (Sundays during August). Free.
Lawnmarket   ☎ 0131 529 4901
www.cac.org.uk

These tours can be a great way to get your bearings in Edinburgh and are especially good for those who have limited time in the city. All tours are hop-on, hop-off, tickets last for 24 hours and there are various discounts for attractions around Edinburgh. Tickets for all tours can be purchased on the bus, from the tourist information office in Princes Mall or from the kiosk on Waverley Bridge. All tours depart from Waverley Bridge.

www.edinburghtour.com

City Sightseeing &

Tours of the city. There is a taped commentary available in nine languages and tours run every 20 minutes during the summer.
Adults £10, concessions available.   ☎ 0131 556 2244

Mac Tours

Tours of the city on a vintage bus, concentrating on the Old Town. There is a live commentary by a trained guide and tours run every 20 minutes during the summer.
Adults £10, concessions available.   ☎ 0131 556 2244

Majestic Tour

Visits Britannia and the Royal Botanic Garden as well as the main city attractions. There is a live commentary by a trained guide and tours run every 20 minutes during the summer.
Adults £10, concessions available.   ☎ 0131 220 0770

The Edinburgh Tour, Guide Friday

Tours the city. There is a live commentary by a trained guide and tours run every 20 minutes during the summer.
Adults £10, concessions available.   ☎ 0131 220 0770

Greyfriars Graveyard

courtesy of Rosemary MacLeod

Auld Reekie Tours

'Terror Tours' travel into the underground vaults with the genuine selection of torture instruments telling tales of torture, trials and executions. 'Underground Tours' tell the supernatural tales of Old Edinburgh in 18th century surroundings. 'Ghost & Torture Tours' feature costumed guides who tell the terrifying true stories of the people who stalked the city (the infamous South Bridge Poltergeist is also visited in the haunted vault).

Daytime and evening tours. 50mins to $1^1/_2$ hours, all leaving from the Tron Kirk on the Royal Mile and there are extra tours around Halloween.

Concessions available.

www.auldreekietours.co.uk ☎ 0131 557 4700

The Cadies and Witchery Tours

The Witchery Tours take a light-hearted look at Edinburgh's darker side including tales of witchcraft, plague and torture. En route you will meet 'jumper ooters' - costumed characters who appear at inopportune times. Tours leave from outside the Witchery restaurant on Castlehill.

Murder and Mystery tour evenings all year. Ghosts and Gore tour evenings during the summer only. Tours last approx $1^1/_2$ hours.

Adults £7.50, concessions available. Booking is essential.

www.witcherytours.com ☎ 0131 225 6745

City of the Dead Tour

Tours wind through the sinister, dark closes of the Old Town, into Greyfriars Graveyard. They then enter the Covenanter's Prison which contains the Black Mausoleum - site of the famous MacKenzie Poltergeist. Tours leave from St. Giles Cathedral on the Royal Mile each evening from Easter to Halloween. Tours last approx $1^1/_4$ hours.

Adults £8.50, concessions available. Not suitable for young children.

www.blackhart.uk.com ☎ 0131 225 9044

Edinburgh Literary Pub Tour

Award-winning tour through Edinburgh's wynds, pubs and 300 years of writing. Tours leave from the Beehive Inn on Grassmarket at 7.30pm. Daily during the summer, check for days during the rest of the year.

Adults £10, concessions available.

www.edinburghliterarypubtour.co.uk ☎ 0800 169 7410

Mercat Tours

Haunted locations, scary stories, eerie underground vaults and history guides. Daytime tours concentrate on Edinburgh's social history whilst evening tours concentrate on Edinburgh's darker side.

Prices, times and start points vary for each tour so telephone or see the website for details.

www.mercattours.com ☎ 0131 225 5445

Emergencies

The freephone numbers to use if someone is in immediate danger, or a crime is being committed, are 999 or 112 (0800 112 999 on Textphone). An operator will ask which service is required; police, ambulance, fire brigade or coastguard. Keep calm, answer their questions clearly and help will soon be with you.

Accidents & ill health

● Entitlement to treatment

Holiday visitors, EU citizens and people from countries with reciprocal arrangements can receive free medical treatment at National Health Service (NHS) hospitals. Non-EU citizens can have free emergency treatment only in the Accident and Emergency (A&E) departments of NHS hospitals; if you need to be admitted to a ward, you will be charged.

The following hospitals have 24 hour A&E departments:
The Royal Hospital for Sick Children   **75 D2**
9 Sciennes Road. For babies and children up to 13. ☎ 0131 536 0000
www.nhslothian.scot.nhs.uk
The Royal Infirmary of Edinburgh at Little France out of map area
51 Little France Crescent, Old Dalkeith Road   ☎ 0131 536 1000
www.nhslothian.scot.nhs.uk

There is a minor injuries unit, open 8am-9pm at
Western General Hospital
Crewe Road South   ☎ 0131 537 1000

● Dentists

Emergency dental treatment can be obtained from
Chalmers Dental Centre
Mon-Fri 9am-9pm. 10am-noon and 7pm-9pm on Saturdays and Sundays. If treatment is needed after 5pm telephone first.
Chalmers Street   ☎ 0131 536 4800

● Doctors & Chemists

If you have a minor illness, either use the 24 hour NHS Direct service (☎ 0845 4647 / www.nhsdirect.nhs.uk), or go to any chemists shop (pharmacy / drugstore) where the pharmacist will be able to help you. The local police station will have a list of doctors in the area and if you need medication after normal closing time (5 to 6pm), they will also have a list of late night chemists.

In Edinburgh some chemists open after 5pm are:

Boots the Chemist Mon-Fri 7.30am to 8pm.
Sat 8am to 6pm. Sun 10.30am to 4.30pm.
46-48 Shandwick Place ☎ 0131 225 6757

Lloyds Pharmacy (inside Waitrose) Mon-Fri 8.30am to 8pm.
Sat 8.30am to 6pm. Sun 11am to 5pm.
38 Comely Bank ☎ 0131 332 5573

Sainsbury's Pharmacy Mon-Sat 9am to 9pm. Sun 10am to 7pm.
Meadowbank Retail Park ☎ 0131 661 1129

Car breakdown

● Breakdown Organisations

If you are not already a member, you can join some breakdown organisations at the roadside, although there may be a surcharge for this service. In the event of a breakdown use the following telephone numbers:

Automobile Association (AA)	www.theaa.com	☎ 0800 88 77 66
Direct Line	www.directline.com	☎ 0800 590 590
Green Flag	www.greenflag.com	☎ 0800 051 0636
More Than	www.morethan.com	☎ 0800 300 988
RAC	www.rac.co.uk	☎ 0800 82 82 82

Lost property

All property handed in to a police station or left in a taxi will be sent to
Lothian & Borders Police HQ **61 D3**
Mon-Fri 9am to 5pm
Fettes Avenue ☎ 0131 311 3131

Enquiries can also be made at
Police Information Centre
10am-7.30pm (6pm Nov-Feb)
Royal Mile, 188 High Street ☎ 0131 226 6966

For property left at other locations:
Edinburgh Airport see pages **78 & 79**
For items lost in the terminal building.
Daily 5.15am to 10.45pm. Charge of £4.50 per item.
www.edinburghairport.com ☎ 0131 344 3486

Waverley Station **4 B1**
Mon-Fri 8am to 5.30pm. Located on platform 1.
Waverley Bridge ☎ 0131 550 2333

Lothian Buses
Mon-Fri 10am to 1.30pm
47 Annandale Street ☎ 0131 558 8858

● Lost or stolen credit cards

Immediately report lost or stolen credit cards to the issuing company:

American Express	www.americanexpress.co.uk	☎ 01273 696 933
Barclaycard	www.barclaycard.co.uk	☎ 0844 811 9111
HSBC	www.hsbc.co.uk	☎ 0845 600 7010
Lloyds TSB	www.lloydstsb.com	☎ 0800 096 9779
Mastercard	www.mastercard.com	☎ 0800 96 4767
NatWest	www.natwest.com	☎ 0870 600 0459
Visa	www.visaeurope.com	☎ 0800 89 1725

Money

● Currency

The pound sterling (£) is the currency for the whole of Britain. It is divided into 100 pence (p). Bank of England banknotes are generally accepted as well as those issued by the Scottish banks. Notes are £1 (only issued by the Royal Bank of Scotland), £5, £10, £20, £50 and £100. The Scottish banknotes are also generally accepted in the rest of Britain but are sometimes viewed with suspicion. Coin values are 1p, 2p, 5p, 10p, 20p, 50p, £1 and £2.

● Banks

Most banks are open on weekdays from 9.30am to 4 or 5pm, and have an ATM (cashpoint). Many main branches are also open for shorter periods on Saturdays.

One branch of each of the major banks is listed below:
Bank of Scotland
Mon-Fri 9am (Wed 9.30am) to 5pm, Sat 10am to 3pm
St James Centre   www.bankofscotland.co.uk   ☎ 0131 456 8751
Royal Bank of Scotland
Mon-Fri 9am (Wed 9.45am) to 4.45pm, Sat 9.15am to 4pm
142/144 Princes Street   www.rbs.co.uk   ☎ 0131 226 2555
Clydesdale Bank
Mon-Fri 9.15am (Wed 9.45am) to 4.45pm, Sat 9am to 1pm
20 Hanover Street   www.cbonline.co.uk   ☎ 0845 782 6302
TSB Scotland
Mon-Fri 9am (Wed 10am) to 5pm (Thurs 6pm), Sat 10am to 6pm
28 Hanover Street   www.lloydstsbscotland.co.uk ☎ 0845 3000 000

● Foreign exchange

The best rates of exchange are usually found in banks or at the airport and the worst rates in hotels. However, Bureau de Change are often open outside banking hours and so may be more convenient.

Thomas Cook
Mon-Fri 9am (Tues 10am) to 6pm (Tues/Sat 5.30pm)
52 Hanover Street ☎ 0845 308 9277
Edinburgh and Scotland Information Centre ☎ 0845 2255 121
3 Princes Street
Edinburgh International Airport ☎ 0870 850 2825
www.edinburghairport.com

● The Euro

Although the UK has not adopted the Euro, many large stores and services will accept it in their larger branches. Look for a sign on the door or ask a member of staff.

● Tax refunds on goods

If you are from a non-EU country, you can reclaim some of the tax you have paid on some of your shopping. Look for a sign 'Tax Free Shopping' in stores. You will need to complete a form and present it with the goods at customs when leaving the UK.

Passports

Photocopy the essential parts of your passport. This may speed things up if it needs to be replaced. If you do lose it or it is stolen, inform the police immediately and contact your embassy or consulate.

● Consulates in Edinburgh

American Consulate
3 Regent Terrace ☎ 0131 556 8315
www.usembassy.org.uk/scotland

Australian Consulate
21-23 Hill Street ☎ 0131 226 8161
www.australia.org.uk

French Consulate
11 Randolph Crescent ☎ 0131 225 7954
www.consulfrance-edimbourg.org

German Consulate
16 Eglinton Crescent ☎ 0131 337 2323
www.edinburgh.diplo.de

Indian Consulate
17 Rutland Square ☎ 0131 229 2144
www.cgiedinburgh.org

Japanese Consulate
2 Melville Crescent ☎ 0131 225 4777
www.edinburgh.uk.emb-japan.go.jp

Russian Federation Consulate
58 Melville Street ☎ 0131 225 7098
www.rusemblon.org

Public toilets

Look out for street signs saying 'toilets' or 'public toilets'. Bear in mind that many are locked after dark, except for the 24 hour unisex variety that look like shiny metal cabins. All other public toilets are separated into male and female and there is sometimes a charge to use them.

Visitors with disabilities

Most buses, trains and stations have disabled facilities and access, but not all. Check in advance before travelling.

National Express www.nationalexpresseastcoast.com
  East Coast   ☎ 0845 722 5225
Lothian Buses www.lothianbuses.com   ☎ 0131 555 6363
Scotrail www.firstgroup.com/scotrail   ☎ 0845 605 7021
Edinburgh and Scotland Information Centre   **4 B1**
Leaflet 'Accessible Scotland' for disabled accommodation.
3 Princes Street   www.edinburgh.org   ☎ 0845 2255 121
Capability Scotland
National advice and information service.
11 Ellersly Road   www.capability-scotland.org.uk ☎ 0131 313 5510

Visitor Information Centres

Visitor Information Centres are able to help with accommodation, visitor attractions, tours, events, timetables and so on. If they do not have the answer, they usually know someone who does.

Edinburgh & Scotland Information Centre   **4 B1**
3 Princes Street   www.edinburgh.org   ☎ 0845 2255 121
Tourist & Airport Information Desk
Edinburgh International Airport   ☎ 0870 040 0007

Getting around

From the airport to the city

Edinburgh International Airport general enquiries.
www.edinburghairport.com   ☎ 0870 0400007
By taxi
There are 3 taxi ranks: private vehicle taxis are at the eastern end of the terminal building, black cabs are next to the coach park and pre-booked taxis are in the short stay multi-storey car park. Many are accessible to wheelchairs. Journey time to the city centre is approximately 25 minutes.
By bus
• Airlink bus number 100 from outside the UK Arrivals to Waverley Railway Station (via the city centre) running every 20 minutes from 5am until 7am and then every 10 minutes until midnight.

• During the night, service N22 runs every 30 minutes.
Journey time of 25 minutes. £3 single £5 return. ☎ 0131 555 6363
www.flybybus.com

Service 35 runs from the airport to Ocean Terminal in Leith every 15 minutes
in the daytime and 30 minutes in the evenings and Sundays. £1 single.
www.lothianbuses.co.uk

The Airdirect 247 service runs from the airport to Inverkeithing Railway
Station and Ferrytoll Park & Ride in Fife. It runs every 20 minutes Mon
to Sat and every hour on Sundays. £4.50 single/day return.
www.airdirect747.com

Edinburgh Shuttle is a fleet of 7 seat minibuses providing a door-to-
door service. Booking is advisable. £9 single. ☎ 0845 500 5000

By car
Take the A8 into the city centre.

Public transport

For information on all public transport within the Lothian area.
Traveline Scotland
www.travelinescotland.com ☎ 0871 200 2233

● Rail

Contact National Rail Enquiries for information about train
times, ticket types and planning your journey.
www.nationalrail.co.uk ☎ 08457 48 49 50

Edinburgh Waverley Station **4 B1**
The main rail station for Edinburgh and the terminus for all
the mainline services. Disabled assistance available.
Waverley Bridge
www.nationalrail.co.uk ☎ 0131 550 2031

Haymarket Station **67 D3**
Many mainline and local services stop here, just over a mile west of
Waverley Station.
Haymarket Terrace
www.nationalrail.co.uk ☎ 0845 601 5929

There are a number of train operators in the Edinburgh area:
National Express East Coast Trains from London, the north-east of
England, Glasgow and Northern Scotland.
www.nationalexpresseastcoaast.com ☎ 08457 225 225
ScotRail Trains throughout Scotland.
www.firstgroup.com/scotrail ☎ 08457 55 00 33
Virgin Trains from south-west England, Glasgow and Aberdeen.
www.virgintrains.co.uk ☎ 08457 222 333

● Tram

Construction has started. Scheduled to be running by 2011.
www.tramtime.com

● Bus/Coach

The bus station on **St. Andrew Square** is the main terminus for all coach services and some bus services. **69 D1**

Lothian Buses
The main within the city. Buy tickets from the bus driver, you must have the correct change, or saver tickets can also be purchased at the Lothian Buses Travelshops.
⭐ except tours & nightbuses

Waverley Bridge,	Mon-Sat 8.15am to 6pm, Sun 9.30am to 5.15pm
Hanover Street,	Mon-Sat 8.15am to 6pm
Shandwick Place,	Mon-Sat 8.15am to 6pm

www.lothianbuses.co.uk ☎ 0131 555 6363
First South East & Central Scotland Bus services in Scotland.
www.firstgroup.com ☎ 0870 8 72 72 71
National Express Coach services throughout Britain.
www.nationalexpress.co.uk ☎ 0870 580 8080
Scottish Citylink Operates coach services throughout Scotland.
⭐ 20% off www.citylink.co.uk ☎ 0870 550 5050

Taxis

Most are the easily recognisable 'Black Cabs'. Only use a taxi licensed to operate in Edinburgh (look for 'Edinburgh No. xxxx' on the passenger door). Never accept a lift from a car touting for business. Instead go to one of the many taxi ranks, telephone for a cab or hail one by waving in the street. Always ask about the fare before travelling.

Central Radio Taxis	www.taxis-edinburgh.co.uk	☎ 0131 229 2468
City Cabs	www.citycabs.co.uk	☎ 0131 228 1211
Computer Cabs	www.comcab-edinburgh.co.uk	☎ 0131 272 8000

Car hire

There is little point driving in Edinburgh itself. Car parks are often full and the one way system needs experience! However, if you intend to travel outside the city hiring a car could be a good idea. Different companies have different requirements, but in most cases you will need to be over 25; you will also require a driving licence. In Scotland, as the rest of Britain, drive on the left hand side of the road. Make sure the company is a member of the British Vehicle Rental and Leasing Association (BVRLA). There are around 30 companies in Edinburgh who are members; see the BVRLA website www.bvrla.co.uk for a full list or telephone ☎ 01494 434747.

A selection of car hire companies is given below:

Avis Rent A Car Ltd	www.avis.co.uk	☎ 0870 153 9103
Europcar UK Ltd	www.europcar.co.uk	☎ 0131 557 3456
Hertz Car Rental	www.hertz.co.uk	☎ 0870 846 0013
National Car Rental	www.nationalcar.co.uk	☎ 0131 453 2580
Thrifty Car Rental	www.thrifty.co.uk	☎ 0131 337 1319

Parking

On the streets, you cannot park AT ANY TIME if there are double yellow lines, a single yellow line means restricted parking at certain times, which will be displayed on a nearby signpost. Illegal parking will result in fines, wheel clamping or towing away of the car. Off street car parks are the best bet, but they do get very busy. The largest ones can be found on Greenside Place, Castle Terrace and Morrison Street.

Park and Ride

There are currently four park and ride sites on the outskirts of Edinburgh (with another just north of the Forth Road Bridge).   **50-51**
www.lothianbuses.co.uk   ☎ 0131 555 6363

Bicycle hire

Edinburgh has an excellent cycle network, making this a good way of seeing the city if you are fit; there are hills! The cycle campaign group Spokes has a lot of information about cycling in and around Edinburgh.   www.spokes.org.uk
Bike Trax
Bike hire from £16 per day. Guided tours are also available.
11-13 Lochrin Place   www.biketrax.co.uk   ☎ 0131 228 6333
Cycle Scotland
Bike hire from £10 per day.
29 Blackfriars Street   www.cyclescotland.co.uk   ☎ 0131 556 5560

Rickshaw

Hire a "greener" form of transport to take the strain from walking some of Edinburgh's steep hills or have a ride just as a treat! They seat up to three but discuss your desired destination and cost before they start cycling.
Pedicabs
During the day the cabs waiting areas are The Mound and Tron Kirk (on the Royal Mile) or in the evening in George Street and Grassmarket. Fare example; Edinburgh Castle to the Palace of Holyroodhouse is £5-£10.
Operating daily.
www.pedicabs.net   ☎ 07876 030203

courtesy of Steve Lloyd

Edinburgh offers every type of accommodation in the book; from luxurious five star hotels to clean, basic backpackers' hostels.

Booking accommodation

If you haven't already booked somewhere to stay, try the **National Information and Booking Service** run by VisitScotland. They have a huge database, including accommodation for disabled visitors. You can book online or at their Visitor Information Centres.

3 Princes Street ☎ 0845 2255 121
www.visitscotland.com

Selected hotels

Listed below are contact details for some of the larger hotels in Edinburgh. Prices can vary depending on special deals, time of booking etc. but a guide to room rates is given.

Rooms available at **£** = up to £80, **££** = £80-120, **£££** = over £120.

Apex Hotels
Contemporary, stylish décor with bar and restaurant facilities. **££**

Apex City, 61 Grassmarket	**4 A1**	☎ 0131 243 3456
Apex European, 90 Haymarket Terrace	**67 D3**	☎ 0131 474 3456
Apex International, 31-35 Grassmarket	**4 A1**	☎ 0131 300 3456
Apex Waterloo Place, 23 Waterloo Place	**70 A1**	☎ 0845 365 0000

www.apexhotels.co.uk

Balmoral Hotel   **4 B1**
Right in the centre, the clock tower makes it a landmark. Stately, baronial but up to date. **£££**
Princes Street ☎ 0131 556 2414
www.thebalmoralhotel.com

Best Western Bruntsfield Hotel   **74 B2**
Attractive Victorian townhouse-style hotel overlooking park/golf course. Comfortable, friendly and stylish. **££**
69 Bruntsfield Place ☎ 0131 229 1393
www.thebruntsfield.co.uk

Caledonian Hilton Hotel   **68 B2**
Large hotel with luxurious Edwardian elegance. Excellent views of the Castle. **£££**
Princes Street ☎ 0131 222 8888
www.caledonian.hilton.com

Carlton Hotel   **4 B1**
On the Royal Mile. Modern interior with good leisure facilities. **££**
North Bridge ☎ 0131 472 3000
www.barcelo-hotels.co.uk

George Hotel 69 **C1**
Close to the shops on the elegant George Street. The refurbishment in 2006 brings this two hundred year old grade II listed building back to a high standard. Fully non-smoking hotel. **££**
19 - 21 George Street ☎ 0131 225 1251
www.edinburghgeorgehotel.co.uk

Holiday Inn Express
Value for money hotels with bar and lounge areas and continental breakfast. **££**

Picardy Place	69 **D1**	☎ 0131 558 2300
300 Cowgate, Royal Mile	5 **C1**	☎ 0131 524 8400
Britannia Way, Ocean Drive, Leith	58 **A2**	☎ 0131 555 4422

www.hiexpress.co.uk

Ibis Hotel 4 **B1**
Almost on the Royal Mile. Breakfasts 4am to noon! **£**
6 Hunter Square ☎ 0131 240 7000
www.ibishotel.com

Macdonald Holyrood Hotel 70 **B2**
Luxurious accommodation and a high standard of service. The Club Floor has a private lounge and butler. **£££**
81 Holyrood Road ☎ 0844 879 9028
www.macdonaldhotels.co.uk

Malmaison Hotel 59 **C2**
In the redeveloped docklands of Leith. Really chic but comfortable rooms, many with views over the water. **£££**
1 Tower Place ☎ 0131 468 5000
www.malmaison-edinburgh.com

Old Waverley Hotel 4 **B1**
Traditional Scottish Hotel almost opposite Waverley Station. **£££**
43 Princes Street ☎ 0131 556 4648
www.oldwaverley.co.uk

Parliament House Hotel 70 **A1**
Quiet, traditional and comfortable. **££**
15 Calton Hill ☎ 0131 478 4000
www.scotland-hotels.co.uk

Premier Inn
Good, basic hotels aiming to provide all you need for a good night's sleep. **£**

1 Morrison Link	68 **A3**	☎ 0870 238 3319
82 Lauriston Place	69 **C3**	☎ 0870 990 6610
51/53 Newhaven Place	57 **D1**	☎ 0870 197 7093

www.premierinn.co.uk

Radisson SAS Hotel   5 **C1**
Large hotel offering modern tasteful accommodation. On the Royal
Mile. **£££**
80 High Street   ☎ 0131 473 6590
www.radissonsas.com

Royal Terrace Hotel   70 **A1**
Class with comfort in this Georgian hotel. Unique terraced gardens
£££
18 Royal Terrace   ☎ 0131 557 3222
www.royalterrace.co.uk

Scotsman Hotel   4 **B1**
Former home of 'The Scotsman' newspaper; now a luxury hotel.
Traditional but state of the art. **£££**
20 North Bridge   ☎ 0131 556 5565
www.thescotsmanhotel.co.uk

Sheraton Grand Hotel   68 **B3**
One of the best of the modern hotels. Central location. **£££**
1 Festival Square   ☎ 0131 229 9131
www.sheraton.com

Travelodge
Good, basic hotels aiming to provide all you need for a good night's
sleep. **£**
Edinburgh Central, 33 St. Mary's Street   5 **C1**   ☎ 0870 191 1637
Edinburgh West End, 69 Belford Road   67 **D2** ☎ 0871 984 6418
www.travelodge.co.uk

In addition to the above, there are many small but superb individual
hotels and guest houses in the city. Contact the Information Centre in
Princes Street.

Budget accommodation
Castle Rock Hostel
Central, big and friendly. Games room with pool table and table tennis.
15 Johnston Terrace   ☎ 0131 225 9666
www.castlerockedinburgh.com

Edinburgh Backpackers Hostel
Dorm and private rooms, self catering kitchens and a café bar.
65 Cockburn Street   ☎ 0131 220 2200
www.hoppo.com

Eglinton Hostel
Located just a few minutes walk from Waverley station and Princes
Street with single, twin and dorm rooms, all of which are en-suite.
9 Haddington Place   ☎ 0870 155 3255
www.syha.org.uk

Edinburgh cuisine ranges from fast food chains to the very best of cosmopolitan fare. You will find meals cooked with fresh Scottish produce at restaurants displaying the 'Taste of Scotland' symbol. A small selection of city centre establishments are listed here.

Restaurants

● Chinese

Dragon Way
Charming restaurant serving Cantonese, Peking and Szechuen dishes. Vibrant Oriental décor. Pre-theatre menu and vegetarian options. Open daily.
74-78 South Clerk Street ☎ 0131 668 1328

J's Modern Chinese Restaurant
Unfussy fresh flavours complement the simplicity and modernity of the décor.
Open daily.
18 Lady Lawson Street ☎ 0131 221 0888

Kweilin
Excellent Cantonese food with seasonal specials. Pleasant, fairly formal atmosphere, leave the children at home perhaps.
Open Tue-Sun.
19-21 Dundas Street ☎ 0131 557 1875
www.kweilin.co.uk

● French

La Garrigue
Recreates the South of France, even on a November day. The food is excellent and the wine list almost entirely from the Languedoc region. Open daily for lunch and dinner.
31 Jeffrey Street ☎ 0131 557 3032
www.lagarrigue.co.uk

Le Café St Honore
Just like a Paris café. The menu here is extensive and mouthwatering. Come early evening for really good value offers.
Open daily.
34 North West Thistle Street Lane ☎ 0131 226 2211

Le Sept
Famous for its crêpes, this long established restaurant has a distinctly French air: friendly, helpful staff and a comfortable relaxed atmosphere.
Open daily, various hours.
5 Hunter Square ☎ 0131 225 5428
www.lesept.co.uk

● Indian

Khukuri Nepalese Restaurant
Despite being named after the knife carried by Gurkhas this is a friendly restaurant with great food. The speciality is Nepalese cuisine but all the usuals from an Indian menu are here too.
8 West Maitland Street ☎ 0131 228 2085
www.thekhukuri.co.uk

Pataka
With its Mackintosh style booths, you can enjoy a traditional or more adventurous meal in peace in this busy Bengali restaurant.
Open daily for lunch and dinner.
190 Causewayside ☎ 0131 668 1167

Suruchi
Authentic Indian cuisine and décor. The food is superb and the proprietor uses Scottish ingredients wherever possible. You may catch live Indian music and dance or jazz.
Open daily for lunch and dinner (no lunch on Sundays).
14a Nicolson Street ☎ 0131 556 6583
www.suruchirestaurant.com

● Italian

Cosmo
Founded 30 years ago, this elegant restaurant balances the best in traditional Italian cuisine, with new and exciting options.
Daily, not Sunday evenings.
58a North Castle Street ☎ 0131 226 6743
www.cosmo-restaurant.co.uk

Pizza Express
There are five restaurants in Edinburgh that are part of the huge chain. All the restaurants have a varied menu but you can be sure that the children will love the pizza.
Open daily, 11.30am to midnight.
23 North Bridge ☎ 0131 557 6411
111 Holyrood Road ☎ 0131 557 5734
Waterview House, The Shore ☎ 0131 554 4332
1 Deanhaugh Street ☎ 0131 332 7229
32 Queensferry Street ☎ 0131 225 8863
www.pizzaexpress.co.uk

Prego
Every authentic Italian dish is freshly prepared in this stylish restaurant.
Closed Sundays, otherwise open lunch times and evenings.
38 St Mary's Street ☎ 0131 557 5754
www.prego-restaurant.com

● Seafood

Creelers
Fresh fish harvested from the west coast, some of it going via the Creelers own smoke house on Arran.
Open daily, closed lunch time Tues and Wed.
3 Hunter Square ☎ 0131 220 4447
www.creelers.co.uk

Fishers in the City
Huge selection of seafood dishes, including marlin and shark. Fresh, well prepared food served by friendly staff in this stylish warehouse.
Open daily.
58 Thistle Street ☎ 0131 225 5109
www.fishersbistros.co.uk

Mussel Inn
Owned and run by shellfish farmers, the produce is as fresh as possible. Go early, it gets very busy.
Open daily.
61-65 Rose Street ☎ 0131 225 5979
www.mussel-inn.com

● Mexican

Coconut Grove
Lively atmosphere and friendly staff make you feel welcome. The food is excellent; be prepared for a long night of enjoyment!
Open daily for lunch and dinner.
3 Lochrin Terrace ☎ 0131 229 1569

Viva Mexico
Run by Mexicans, frequented by everybody, this friendly, buzzing restaurant is one of the few to serve perfectly cooked calamare, along with many other traditional and imaginative dishes.
Open daily for lunch and dinner (no lunch on Sundays).
41 Cockburn Street ☎ 0131 226 5145
www.viva-mexico.co.uk

● Scottish

Dubh Prais
Dubh Prais offers the best in traditional Scottish cuisine, simply but beautifully and imaginatively cooked, in a homely atmosphere.
Closed Sun/Mon.
123b High Street ☎ 0131 557 5732
www.dubhpraisrestaurant.com

Grain Store
Flexible menu allows a selection of lunchtime 'lite bites' or traditional courses. Seasonal specialities. Unpretentious but top-drawer cuisine. Open daily.
30 Victoria Street ☎ 0131 225 7635
www.grainstore-restaurant.co.uk

Sizzling Scot Steakhouse & Grill
The original Sizzling Scot Steakhouse offering traditional Scottish cuisine using fresh local produce in a relaxed and friendly environment.
Open daily (closed for lunch Sun/Mon).
103-105 Dalry Road ☎ 0131 337 7744
www.sizzlingscot.co.uk

● Spanish

Igg's
A contemporary blend of Scottish ingredients with a Spanish twist. Tasteful décor with classical guitar music. Not cheap, but top class. Closed Sun.
15 Jeffrey Street ☎ 0131 557 8184

● Vegetarian

David Bann's Vegetarian Restaurant
Cosmopolitan, tasty veggie food in a pleasant, modern atmosphere. Open daily, 11am to at least midnight.
56-58 St Mary's Street ☎ 0131 556 5888
www.davidbann.com

Henderson's Salad Table
Their motto is 'Eat better, Live better'. Local organic food, GM free with no artificial ingredients. Brilliant vegetarian food and live music. Open daily, 8am to 10.45pm.
94 Hanover Street ☎ 0131 225 2131
www.hendersonsofedinburgh.co.uk

Cafés

Café at the Palace see page 7

Clarinda's Tearoom
A 'proper' tearoom; doilies, ornaments and a groaning cake trolley.
Mon to Sat 9am to 4.45pm, Sun from 10am.
69 Canongate ☎ 0131 557 1888

Made in France
All the food is imported from France, from the baguettes to the coffee.
Mon to Fri 9.30am to 5pm, Sat 10am to 4pm.
5 Lochrin Place ☎ 0131 221 1184
www.madeinfrance.co.uk

Pret A Manger
This fast food chain has adopted a policy of high quality, contemporary,
well presented good food, including wraps, sushi and soup.
Open daytimes, Mon-Sat.
56 Shandwick Place
25 Castle Street
51 Hanover Street
www.pret.com

Spoon
Contemporary and stylish, Spoon offers an upmarket twist to the usual
sandwich, soup and cake. The ingredients are top quality and fresh.
9am to 5pm. Closed Sun.
15 Blackfriars Street ☎ 0131 556 6922

The Elephant House
With over 600 elephants to amuse the children, this popular, large
café is a good place to relax and enjoy a substantial snack and
steaming coffee.
8am to 10pm (slightly different at weekends).
21 George IV Bridge ☎ 0131 220 5355
www.elephant-house.co.uk

Uncle T's
A unique sandwich bar where you can sit down and take your time.
Interesting selection of Tunisian-based fare as well as jacket potatoes.
Mon to Fri 8am to 7pm. Sat 10am to 6pm, closed Sun.
8 Forrest Road ☎ 0131 226 1539

Valvona & Crolla Caffè Bar
Gem that has built up a reputation for superb Mediterranean cuisine
over the past 70 years. Busy most of the time so book.
Mon to Sat 8am to 6pm, closed Sun.
19 Elm Row ☎ 0131 556 6066
www.valvonacrolla.co.uk

Pubs & bars

Barony Bar
Traditional, relaxed pub, good ale plus whisky and a real fire in winter.
81-85 Broughton Street ☎ 0131 557 0546

Bert's Bar
Watch a game of rugby on a big screen and sink a pint of good ale with a tasty pie.
Raeburn Place ☎ 0131 332 6345

Bow Bar
Traditional pub which concentrates on good ale. Good place for a nice quiet pint.
80 West Bow ☎ 0131 226 7667
www.bowbar.com

Café Royal
Worth a visit to see the Doulton tiled walls alone. Central Island bar serving good ales and beers. Oyster bar upstairs.
17 West Register Street ☎ 0131 556 1884

El Barrio
Latin Cocktail Bar and Club offering infamous cocktails and dance floor. Open 10pm to 3am daily.
119 Rose Street ☎ 0131 226 4311
www.elbarrio.co.uk

Frankenstein
Gothic, monster décor with appropriately named cocktails. Be prepared for some (moderately) scary surprises! Loud music and good fun.
26 George IV Bridge ☎ 0131 622 1818
www.frankenstein-pub.co.uk

Great Grog Wine Bar
Run by a wine merchant company of the same name, you can sip wine by candlelight while relaxing on comfortable sofas.
43 Rose Street ☎ 0131 225 1616
www.greatgrog.co.uk

Guildford Arms
Real ale free house built in 1898 still showing late Victorian opulence including a Jacobean style ceiling. Also view it from mezzanine level in the "Gallery" restaurant.
1-5 West Register Street ☎ 0131 556 4312
www.guildfordarms.com

The Filling Station
An American themed bar and restaurant with the bar overlooking the High Street.
233-241 High Street ☎ 0131 226 2488

The Jolly Judge
For a huge selection of whiskies, this pub takes some beating. A warm log fire in the winter and low beamed ceilings make this a cosy retreat.
7 James Court   ☎ 0131 225 2669
www.jollyjudge.co.uk

The Royal McGregor
Actually run by the McGregor family, this pub serves the best of traditional drinks (ales and whiskies) alongside cocktails and shots.
154 High Street   ☎ 0131 225 7064
www.theroyalmcgregor.co.uk

Shopping

Shops are generally open from 9am until 6pm, with late night opening (until 8 or 9pm) generally on a Thursday and shorter hours on a Sunday.

The main shopping street is Princes Street, where you'll find all the usual High Street stores and the larger department stores of Frasers, Debenhams, Marks & Spencer and Jenners. Rose Street and George Street, parallel to Princes Street, have more upmarket shops. The Royal Mile has plenty of gift shops and amongst the traditional souvenirs there are many good quality products. On and around Grassmarket there is a good range of antique, arts and crafts, book and other speciality shops.

Victoria Street from Grassmarket

courtesy of Sonia Dawkins

Shopping centres

Multrees Walk
69 D1

Home to Harvey Nichols and an exclusive designer boulevard adjacent to the St James Shopping Centre
St Andrew Square ☎ 0131 557 0050
www.the-walk.co.uk

Ocean Terminal
58 B1

Over 60 High Street stores, a 12 screen cinema, bars and restaurants are to be found in Ocean Terminal. The Royal Yacht Britannia is moored alongside. Transgression Park is an urban freesports facility on the top floor of the shopping centre.
Open daily, until 8pm on weekdays, Sat 7pm, Sun 6pm, the bars, restaurants and cinema are open until midnight.
Ocean Drive, Leith ☎ 0131 555 8888
www.oceanterminal.com

Princes Mall
4 B1

There are over 40 shops and a food court in this smart underground shopping centre next to Waverley station. Open daily.
Princes Street ☎ 0131 557 3759
www.princesmall-edinburgh.co.uk

St. James Shopping
69 D1

Undercover shopping centre at the east end of Princes Street. Over 50 High Street stores, including John Lewis, and a food court.
Open daily.
Leith Street ☎ 0131 557 0050
www.stjamesshopping.com

Large department stores

Harvey Nichols

Well known for stocking designer clothes and speciality foods in its Foodmarket. Open daily.
Multrees Walk, 30-34 St. Andrew Square ☎ 0131 524 8388
www.harveynichols.com

Jenners

One of Britain's oldest department stores, it has been in its current position on Princes Street since 1838. Worth a visit for the old-fashioned courtesy and décor alone, Jenners has designer labels and a sumptuous food hall. Open daily.
48 Princes Street ☎ 0131 225 2442
www.jenners.com

John Lewis
Edinburgh's largest department store with far reaching views from the café and restaurant.
69 St James Shopping Centre   ☎ 0131 556 9121
www.johnlewis.com

Scottish products

Geoffrey (Tailor) Kiltmakers
One of the best places to buy or hire off-the-peg or made-to-measure Highland Dress. 21st Century Kilts offers contemporary stylish kilts in a variety of materials including denim and leather. Open daily.
57-59 High Street   ☎ 0131 557 0256
www.geoffreykilts.co.uk

Peckham's
Licensed delicatessen. The place to buy MacSween's award-winning haggis, considered to be the best in the world. Open daily until midnight, Sun 11pm.
155-159 Bruntsfield Place   ☎ 0131 229 7054
www.peckhams.co.uk

Royal Mile Whiskies
Specialises in single malt scotch whisky, although also stocks blended whisky, Irish whiskey and bourbon whiskey. Open daily.
379 High Street   ☎ 0131 225 3383
www.royalmilewhiskies.com

Scottish Gems
Huge selection of Celtic jewellery. Closed Sunday.
162 Morningside Road   ☎ 0131 447 5579
www.scottish-gems.co.uk

Cockburn Street   courtesy of Sonia Dawkins

There's plenty to see in Edinburgh even when the festivals aren't on. To find out what's on and where, see *The List* www.list.co.uk published fortnightly on a Thursday, or the *Edinburgh Evening News* www.edinburghnews.scotsman.com which is published daily.

Cinemas

Like all big cities Edinburgh has a wide choice of cinemas; from the multiplexes with the latest equipment and auditoriums to the smaller independent cinemas showing more unusual films.

Cameo Cinema ♿   74 **B1**
Independent cinema. Specialises in new art-house films and late night showings of cult films. Bar.
38 Home Street   ☎ 0131 228 2800
www.picturehouses.co.uk

Cineworld Cinema ♿   74 **A1**
Shows the popular new releases.
FountainPark, 130-133 Dundee Street   ☎ 0871 200 2000
www.cineworld.co.uk

Dominion Cinema ♿   74 **B3**
Old fashioned independent cinema showing the latest mainstream films. Café / Bar.
18 Newbattle Terrace   ☎ 0131 447 4771
www.dominioncinemas.net

Filmhouse Cinema ♿   68 **B3**
An eclectic mix of independent, classic and art-house films from around the world shown in a converted church. Café / Bar.
88 Lothian Road   ☎ 0131 228 2688
www.filmhousecinema.com

Odeon Cinema ♿   68 **B3**
Shows the latest releases. Bar.
118 Lothian Road   ☎ 0871 22 44 007
www.odeon.co.uk

Vue Cinema ♿
Two cinemas each with 12 screens showing the latest mainstream films.
Omni, Greenside   **70 A1**   ☎ 08712 240 240
Ocean Terminal, Ocean Drive, Leith   **58 B1**   ☎ 08712 240 240
www.myvue.com

Theatres and concert halls

During the Festivals all kinds of venues are transformed into theatres but listed here are those with performances all year round.

Assembly Rooms Theatre ♿ **4 A1**
Popular venue during the Fringe Festival also hosts regular ceilidhs, dances and gigs.
54 George Street ☎ 0131 220 4348
www.assemblyroomsedinburgh.co.uk

Bedlam Theatre ♿ **4 B2**
Home to Edinburgh University Theatre Company, this theatre is run by students but also has shows from other theatre companies too.
11b Bristo Place ☎ 0131 225 9893
www.bedlamtheatre.co.uk

Church Hill Theatre ♿ **74 B3**
Morningside Road ☎ 0131 447 7597
www.edinburgh.gov.uk

Dance Base **4 A2**
14-16 Grassmarket ☎ 0131 225 5525
www.dancebase.co.uk

Festival Theatre ♿ **5 C2**
At the heart of the International Festival and the stage for Scottish Opera and Ballet.
13-29 Nicolson Street ☎ 0131 529 6000
www.eft.co.uk

Gateway Theatre **64 A3**
42 Elm Row, Leith Walk ☎ 0131 317 3939

King's Theatre ♿ **74 B1**
Offers the most eclectic mix in the city, from productions by major theatre touring companies to Shakespeare to pantomime.
2 Leven Street ☎ 0131 529 6000
www.eft.co.uk

Playhouse Theatre ♿ **70 A1**
Stages West End musicals for most of the year as well as pop concerts.
18-22 Greenside Place ☎ 0870 606 3424
www.edinburghplayhouse.org.uk

Queen's Hall Theatre ♿ **76 A1**
Hosts a lively programme of concerts from chamber music to rock, from jazz to opera. Home of the Scottish Chamber Orchestra.
Clerk Street ☎ 0131 668 2019
www.thequeenshall.net

Ross Open Air Theatre   **4 A1**
Princes Street Gardens   ☎ 0131 228 8616
www.edinburgh.gov.uk

Royal Lyceum Theatre ♿   **68 B3**
Resident Royal Lyceum Company directs classic and contemporary
plays.
Grindlay Street   ☎ 0131 248 4848
www.lyceum.org.uk

Traverse Theatre ♿   **68 B3**
Exciting, original and innovative new works by contemporary writers.
10 Cambridge Street   ☎ 0131 228 1404
www.traverse.co.uk

Usher Hall ♿   **68 B3**
Base for the Scottish National Orchestra and has concerts by
orchestras, musicians and singers.
Lothian Road   ☎ 0131 228 1155
www.usherhall.co.uk

Comedy Clubs
Jongleurs
Comedy shows on Fridays and Saturdays (and occasionally
weeknights) followed by music and dancing until 3am.
Omni, Greenside Place   ☎ 0844 844 0044
www.jongleurs.com

The Stand
Stand up shows featuring a team of comperes, a beginner's spot and
acts selected from the best Scottish and international comedians.
5 York Place   ☎ 0131 558 72 72
www.thestand.co.uk

Edinburgh at night

©Domhnall Dods

Live music venues

You can hear live music, of one sort or another, most nights in the hundreds of pubs in the city. Some of the best venues are as follows:

©U.P.images_photo

Bannermans
Bands perform most nights in the vaulted cellars of an original tenement.
212 Cowgate ☎ 0131 556 3254
www.bannermansgigs.co.uk

Jazz Centre
A converted church, recently renovated, that has live jazz music most nights of the week.
4-6 Grassmarket ☎ 0131 473 2000
www.jazzcentre.co.uk

The Liquid Room
Popular venue with visiting and local indie and R&B bands. Big names play here occasionally to packed crowds.
9c Victoria Street ☎ 0131 225 2564
www.liquidroom.com

The Royal Oak
Regular folk music sessions.
1 Infirmary Street ☎ 0131 557 2976

Whistlebinkies
Live entertainment, rock, pop and folk music every night of the week until 3am.
4-6 South Bridge ☎ 0131 557 5114
www.whistlebinkies.com

Clubs

The club scene in Edinburgh has an eclectic mix of music styles and many clubs will have different music each night, the bigger ones will have different styles on different floors. The popular clubs and the music they play changes regularly so check *The List* for what's on and where. Most of Edinburgh's nightlife is around Grassmarket, Cowgate, Lothian Road, Broughton Street and in the West End. Most of the city centre clubs stay open until 3am.

Since the late 1940s Edinburgh has been a hotbed for artistic talent, beginning with the International Festival and the Festival Fringe. The summer programme has now grown to include the Military Tattoo, the Film Festival, the Book Festival, the Jazz and Blues Festival and the Mela. Combined, these festivals tend to be referred to as The Festival. They cover a huge range of performance styles and venues and are probably the largest and most prestigious arts festivals in the world. For information on all Edinburgh's festivals see:
www.edinburghfestivals.co.uk

● Edinburgh International Festival

Started in 1947 this is the festival that got it all started. A mix of opera, classical music, ballet and theatre performed by international stars in some of the city's biggest venues. The most popular events can be sold out just days after tickets go on sale. The festival culminates in a spectacular fireworks concert in Princes Street Gardens, although the fireworks can be seen from vantage points all over the city.

The Hub, Castle Hill   4 A2
www.eif.co.uk   ☎ 0131 473 2000

● Edinburgh Festival Fringe

By far the largest of all the festivals, the Fringe has around 15,000 performances spread across 200 venues within Edinburgh. Performances go on around the clock and late night licensed premises dominate the festival scene. Many of Britain's leading comedians, performers and actors enjoyed their first success here. Fringe Sunday (always the second Sunday of the festival) is a huge, free, open-air event in Holyrood Park which enables festival-goers to see snippets of lots of different shows.

The Fringe Office, 180 High Street
www.edfringe.com   ☎ 0131 226 0026

● Edinburgh Military Tattoo

Featuring pipes and drums, massed military bands, display teams, dancers and acts from around the world set against the backdrop of Edinburgh Castle. Tickets need to be booked well in advance. Seats are in the open and as no performance has as yet been cancelled due to inclement weather it is wise to have wet weather gear with you! The late performance on a Saturday is followed by a fireworks display.

The Tattoo Office, 32 Market Street   4 B1
Tickets range in price from about £10 to £30.
Evening performances daily with an early evening showing on Saturday.
www.edintattoo.co.uk   ☎ 0131 225 1188

● Edinburgh International Film Festival

The longest running film festival in the world with a worldwide reputation. A chance to preview mainstream and independent new releases and attend interviews, discussions and debates with those working in the film industry.

Filmhouse, 88 Lothian Road   **68 B3**
www.edfilmfest.org.uk   ☎ 0131 228 4051 or
                                        ☎ 0131 623 8030 (ticket hotline)

● Edinburgh International Book Festival

Based in Charlotte Square Gardens the book festival has discussions, readings, lectures, debates and workshops with some of the world's leading authors. The Children's programme runs alongside and has grown to become a showcase for children's writers and illustrators.

Scottish Book Centre, 137 Dundee Street
www.edbookfest.co.uk   ☎ 0131 718 5666

● Edinburgh International Jazz and Blues Festival

The longest running jazz festival in the UK has local and international jazz artists playing at venues which range from concert halls to pubs.

29 St. Stephens Street
www.edinburghjazzfestival.co.uk

● Edinburgh Mela

Scotland's biggest inter-cultural event celebrates with music, colour, dance, art, fashion, food, children's activities and the Mela bazaar. Tickets can be purchased in advance for ticketed events from Usher Hall.

The Arts Quarter, Gateway Theatre, Elm Row   **64 A3**
www.edinburgh-mela.co.uk   ☎ 0131 557 140

Military Tattoo

courtesy of Edinburgh & Lothians Tourist Board

● January

Burns' Night 25th January

To celebrate the birthday of Scottish poet Robert Burns. Traditional Burns' Suppers of haggis, neeps and tatties are served at pubs and restaurants throughout the city.

● February

Six Nations Rugby Feb-Mar

Annual competition between the rugby union teams of Scotland, England, Wales, Ireland, France and Italy. At least two of Scotland's games will be played at Murrayfield.

Scottish Rugby Union, Murrayfield Stadium ☎ 0131 346 5000
www.scottishrugby.org

● March

Ceilidh Culture Mar-Apr

A celebration of traditional scottish arts with music, dancing, poetry and storytelling.

www.ceilidhculture.co.uk ☎ 0131 228 1155

● April

Edinburgh International Science Festival Two weeks at Easter

Shows, workshops, presentations, hands-on activities and exhibitions on all things 'science'; designed to inspire, stimulate and entertain.

4 Gayfield Place Lane ☎ 0131 558 7666
www.sciencefestival.co.uk

● May

Imaginate Festival Last week of May

The world's leading theatre companies perform shows for children aged 3 to 12. Book tickets at Traverse Theatre Box Office.

45a George Street ☎ 0131 228 1404
www.imaginate.org.uk

● June

Royal Highland Show Four days in June

A four-day festival showcasing rural and agricultural life and is Scotland's largest outdoor event with over 150,000 visitors each year, 1000 exhibitors and 4000 animals. It is held at the Royal Highland Centre Showground at Ingliston.

www.royalhighlandshow.org ☎ 0131 333 5236

Edinburgh International Film Festival Varies, June-Aug

See page 47 for details.

● July

Edinburgh International Jazz and Blues Festival
See page 47 for details.   **Last week of July, first week of August**

● August

Edinburgh Festival Fringe
See page 46.   **Three weeks in August**

Edinburgh Military Tattoo
See page 46.   **Three weeks in August**

Edinburgh International Book Festival
See page 47.   **Second half of August**

Edinburgh International Festival
See page 46.   **Last three weeks of August**

Edinburgh Mela   **Last week of August**
See page 47.

courtesy of Rosemary MacLeod

● September

Doors Open Day   **Weekends in September**
For one day only step inside and explore a wide variety of buildings
whose distinguished, colourful or unusual interiors are rarely open to
the public.
www.doorsopendays.org.uk   ☎ 0131 557 8686

● December

Capital Christmas   **Throughout December**
Christmas celebrations centred around Princes Street Gardens
beginning with the switching on of the Christmas Lights.
www.edinburghchristmas.com   ☎ 0131 529 3914

Edinburgh's Hogmanay   **29th December - 1st January**
Four days of celebrations to welcome in the new year. Many events
are free but tickets are required for some. Access to the party on
Princes Street for the night of the 31st requires a pass.
Edinburgh's Hogmanay Box Office,
The Hub, Castlehill   ☎ 0131 473 2000
www.edinburghshogmanay.org

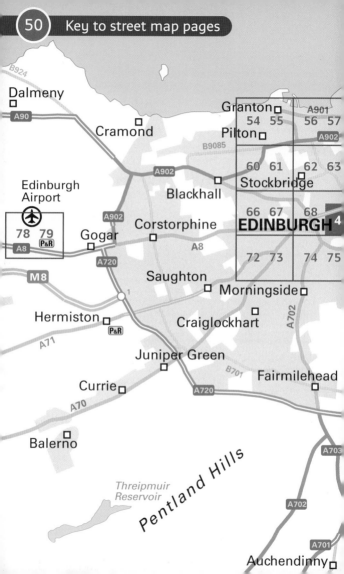

B924

Dalmeny

A90

Cramond

Edinburgh
Airport ✈

Gogar

A902

A8

M8

Hermiston
P&R

A71

Currie

A70

Balerno

Threipmuir
Reservoir

Granton
A901

54 55   56 57

Pilton
A902

B9085

60 61   62 63

Blackhall

Stockbridge

Corstorphine

66 67   68

A8

EDINBURGH 4

Saughton

72 73   74 75

Morningside

A702

Craiglockhart

Juniper Green

B701

Fairmilehead

A720

A703

Pentland Hills

A702

A701

Auchendinny

78 79 P&R

FIRTH OF FORTH

58 59
Leith
A199
64 65
Meadowbank
Portobello
A1
71
Duddingston
Musselburgh
A19
Newcraighall
B1348
5
Wallyford
76 77
A6095
P&R
A1
A1
A7
A6106
Millerhill
Liberton
A701
Gilmerton
P&R
A720
B701
A720
Dalkeith
A68
Eskbank
Loanhead
Bonnyrigg
and Lasswade
Bilston
B704
A6094
A7
Roslin
Newtongrange
Arniston

A720	Primary road dual / single carriageway
A70	'A' Road dual / single carriageway
B701	'B' Road dual / single carriageway
	Other road dual / single carriageway
→	One-way street / Restricted access street
	Pedestrian street
	Minor road / Track
FB	Footpath / Cycle path / Footbridge
⧧ ⊛	Railway station
	Tram (under construction)
●	Bus / Coach station
P	Car Park
	Building open to the public
	Shopping centre / Supermarket
	Education
	Hospital / Health centre
	Other important building

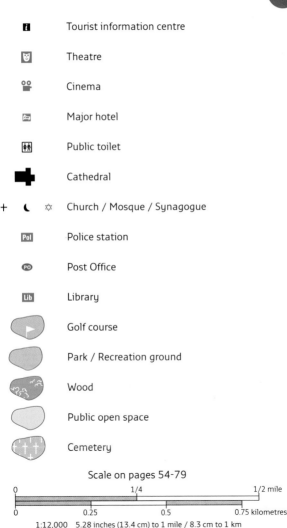

i		Tourist information centre
		Theatre
		Cinema
		Major hotel
		Public toilet
		Cathedral
+ ☾ ✡		Church / Mosque / Synagogue
Pol		Police station
PO		Post Office
Lib		Library
		Golf course
		Park / Recreation ground
		Wood
		Public open space
		Cemetery

Scale on pages 54-79

0		1/4		1/2 mile
0	0.25		0.5	0.75 kilometres

1:12,000 5.28 inches (13.4 cm) to 1 mile / 8.3 cm to 1 km

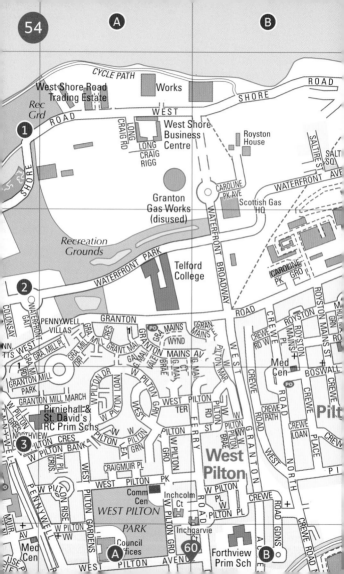

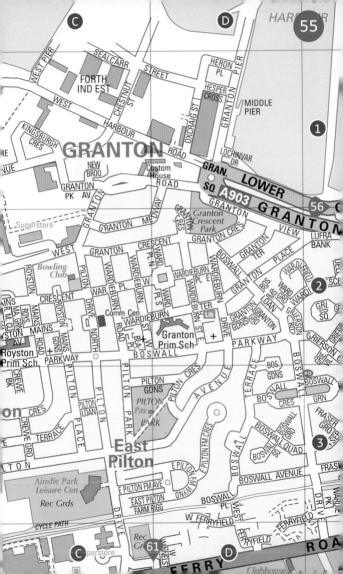

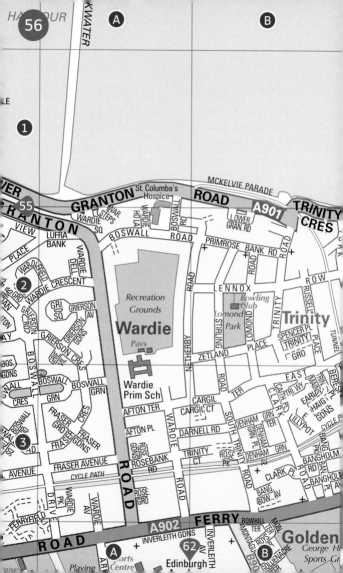

WESTERN HARBOUR
WESTERN HARBOUR DRIVE
W. HARBOUR WAY
W. HARBOUR PL
WESTERN HARBOUR DRIVE
Development

Next Generation Club

Premier Inn

Lighthouse

NEWHAVEN HARBOUR

Newhaven Heritage Mus

NEWHAVEN PLACE

WINDRUSH DRIVE
SANDPIPER RD
GLEN

OCEAN DR

1

Mill

58

PIER PL LINDSAY RD

Victoria Prim Sch

STARBANK RD

NEWHAVEN MAIN ST

AND NEW AUCH
WD CT **1** CT

WILLOW ROW

ANNFIELD
GT
NEW LA
ANNFIELD ST

ANCH
A901
LINDS

Star-bank Park

LAVEROCK AVE
LAVEROCK CR
LAVEROCKBANK TER
CRAIGHALL BANK TER

PARK
PK PL
PARK RD
SOUTH PK
DERBY
BELVUE
ROAD

WILLOW ROW

JESSFIELD TER
HAWTHORNVALE

NICHOLLFIELD

NORTH

NEWHAVEN

2

LAVER
MAY GDNS
LAVEROCK GRO
ROSEVILLE GDNS
MAY GDNS
ROAD

STANLEY ROAD
WEST
CHERRYBANK

DUDLEY CRES
DUDLEY TER
DUDLEY GRO
DUDLEY GDNS

DUDLEY BK
HUTH

Comm Cen

Bowling Club

TRINITY
BERESFORD GDNS
Med Cen
UXMOUNT

CRAIGHALL CRES
GRAND
VILLE

Trinity Academy

CRAIGHALL AV

Trinity Prim Sch

SUMMERSIDE
SUMMERSIDE PLACE

Fort Prim Sch

UXMOUNT
GRANDFIELD

CRAIGHALL GDNS

CRAIGHALL BK

CYCLE PATH

Bowling Club

VICTORIA PARK

ROAD

Med Cen

Pavs
Bangholm Rec Grd

CRAIGHALL TER

CYCLE PATH

PK NEUK

VICTORIA

BONNINGTON TER

TRANS SAR
PITT

3

CLARK AVENUE

BANGH GRO
BANGH LOAN
BANGHOLM

Holy Cross RC Prim Sch

ROAD A902 FERRY

CHANCE
CHANCELOT
BOWAR PL

NEW

CONNAUGHT
GOSFORD

BONNINGTON
GRO **1**

BONNINGTON AV

GRAHAM ST

CYC

Med Cen

Pav
acre
eriot's
ound

EASTER WARRISTON

WARRISTON ROAD
CHANCELOT
CRES
CYCLE PATH

Lethem Pk
DALMENY RD
CONNAUGHT

ARNEH
CONNAUGHT PL

WHITINGFORD
MILNACRE

Bonning
Ind Est

Crematorium

63

Allotments

BEACHFIELD
BONNYHAUGH
WARTFIELD
BONNY

ELIZ

C

D

LADEHEAD

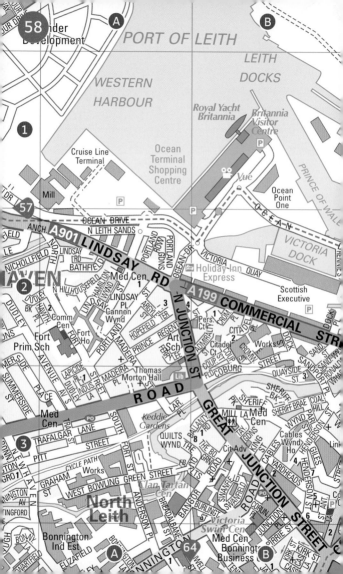

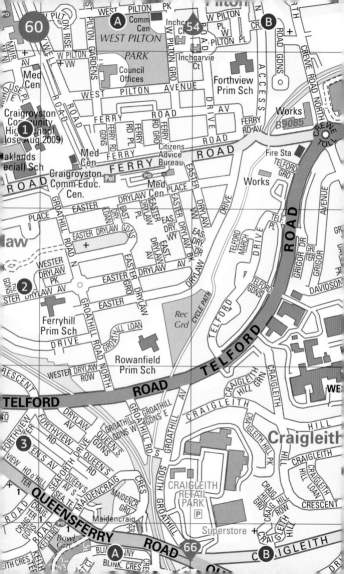

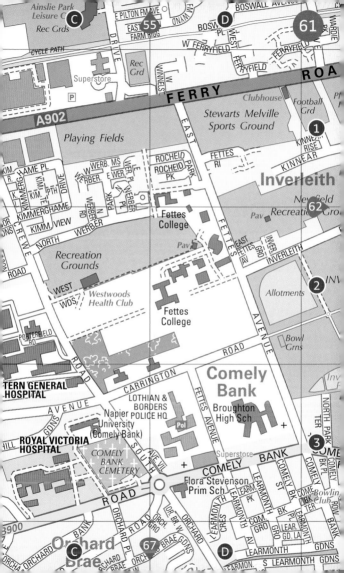

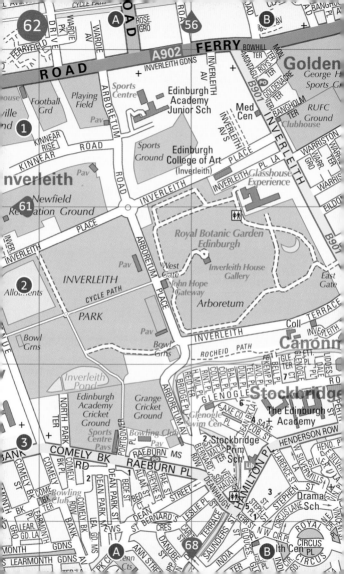

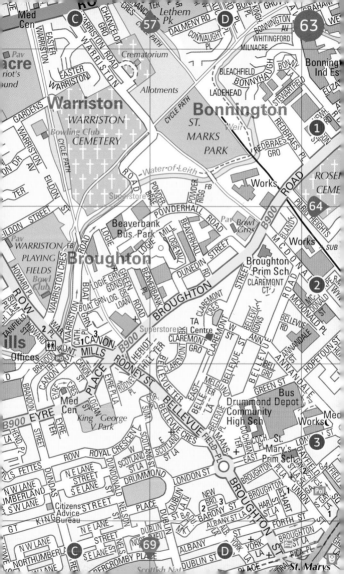

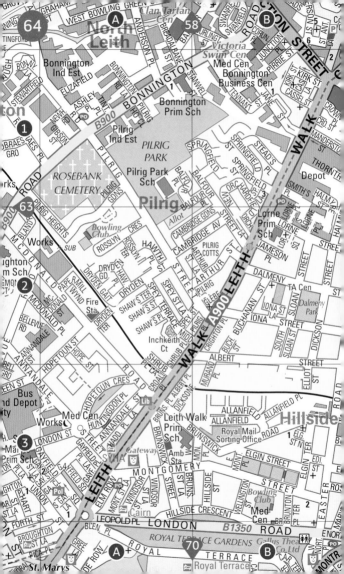

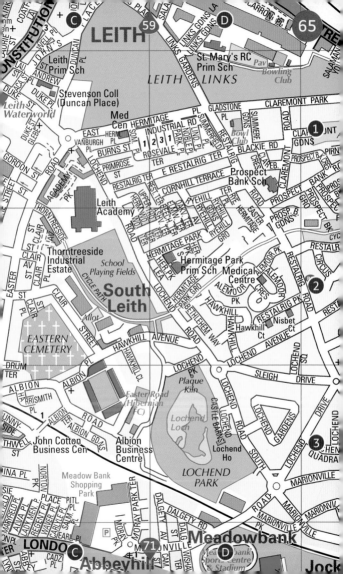

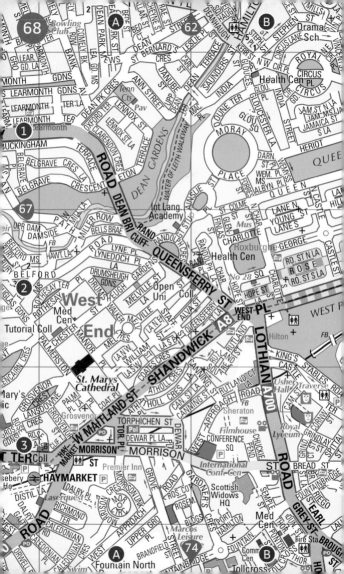

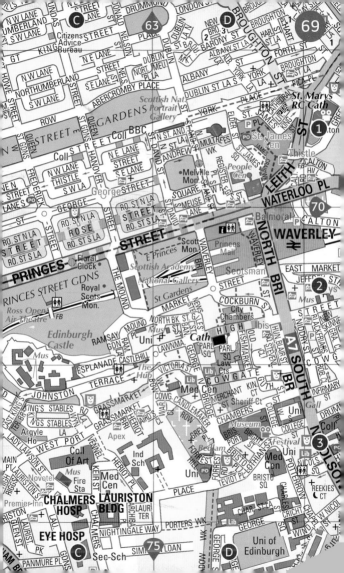

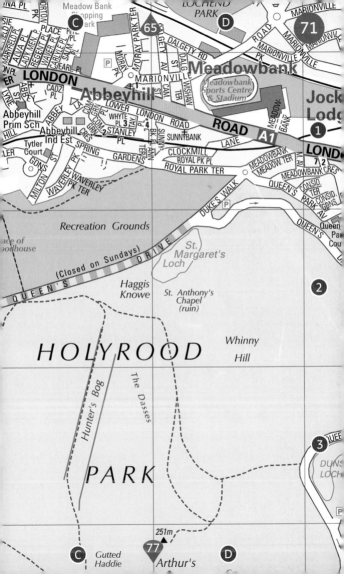

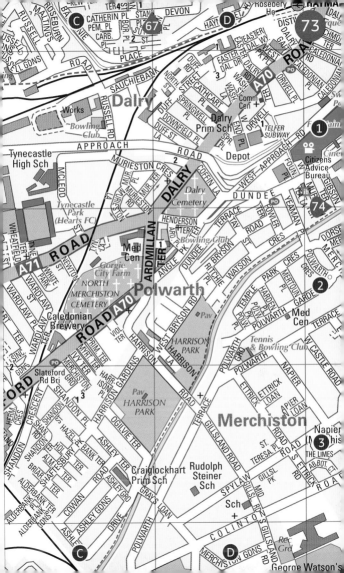

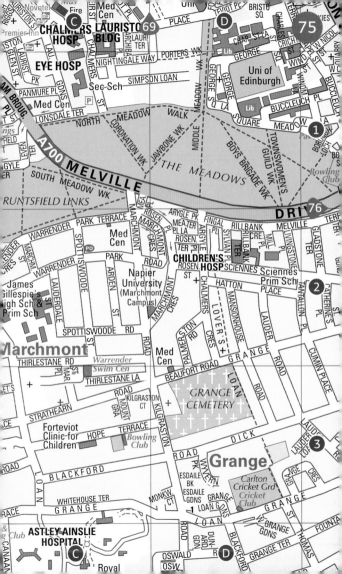

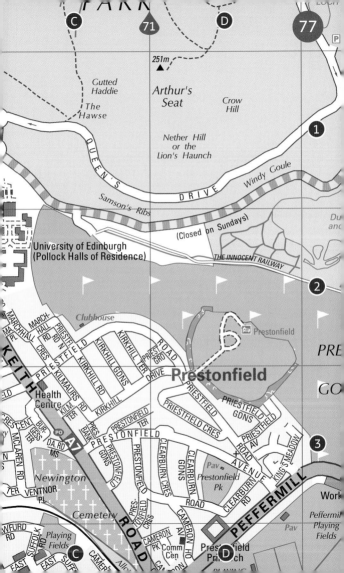

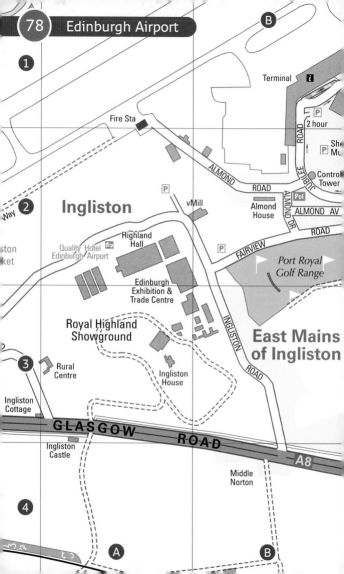

EDINBURGH AIRPORT
(Turnhouse)

JUBILEE ROAD

BURNSIDE ROAD

GOGAR BRIDGE RD

t stay &
i-storey

P Car Hire

P Long stay

P Long stay

P Staff

General Aviation Terminal

Gogar Mains

Hilton

EASTFIELD ROAD

East Ingliston House

P Long Stay

P Long Stay

P&R

Ingliston Park & Ride

Gogar Stone

GOGARSTONE

GLAS

GOGA COLE

How to use this index

This index combines entries for street names, place names and tourist features. Street names are shown in black type e.g. Princes Street. Place names are shown in capital letters e.g. HAYMARKET. Tourist features are shown in blue type e.g. Edinburgh Castle.

All entries are followed by a map reference e.g. 67 B2 which means that the feature can be found on page 67 in grid square B2.

Some names are followed by a number in bold e.g. **3**. These numbers can be found on the map where there is insufficient space to show the name in full. There is also a list of all these numbered streets on page 96.

General abbreviations

App	Approach	Dr	Drive	La	Lane	S	South
Arc	Arcade	E	East	Ln	Loan	Sq	Square
Av	Avenue	Est	Estate	Lwr	Lower	St	Street
Bk	Bank	Fm	Farm	Mkt	Market	Sub	Subway
Bowl	Bowling	Fld	Field	Ms	Mews	Ter	Terrace
Br / Bri	Bridge	Gdn	Garden	Mid	Middle	Trd	Trading
Bdy	Broadway	Gdns	Gardens	N	North	Vw	View
Bldgs	Buildings	Gra	Grange	Par	Parade	Vil	Villa
Cen	Central, Centre	Grd	Ground	Pk	Park	Vil	Villas
Circ	Circus	Grn	Green	Pl	Place	Wk	Walk
Cl	College	Gro	Grove	Pt	Point	W	West
Coll	Corner	Hts	Heights	Quad	Quadrant	Wf	Wharf
Cotts	Cottages	Ho	House	Ri	Rise	Wd	Wood
Ct	Court	Hos	Houses	Rd	Road	Wds	Woods
Cres	Crescent	Ind	Industrial	St.	Saint		
Cft	Croft	Junct	Junction	Sch	School		

Place name abbreviations

Inglis. Ingliston   Newbr. Newbridge

84

93